upload

upload
Copyright © 2018 by Lauren Berenjy

All rights reserved.
Produced in the United States of America.
No part of this book may be used, reproduced or
replicated in any form without written permission, except
brief quotations and/or excerpts for review purposes.
www.berenjy.com

ISBN: 978-1-72-889021-0

Title: _____

Pre-Production
- ☐ topics » outline » script
- ☐ SEO research

Production
- ☐ prep set
- ☐ film movie
- ☐ film b-roll
- ☐ create thumbnail
- ☐ crate social media content

Post-Production
- ☐ edit: lighting
- ☐ edit: transitions
- ☐ edit: sound
- ☐ insert: branded intro
- ☐ insert: branded outro
- ☐ rename video file + thumbnail for upload

Upload
- ☐ SEO + LSI keywords
- ☐ front load keywords in title
- ☐ create description
- ☐ top tags (top channel names as last keywords)
- ☐ create time stamps for long videos
- ☐ add video to playlists
- ☐ monetize + categorize
- ☐ add social hook
- ☐ add end screens + cards

Engagement
- ☐ like + comment on video
- ☐ share to all social media
- ☐ comment on related content

Outline: *What's my angle?*

- [ ] First 15 Seconds:

- [ ] **Branded Intro**
- [ ] Greet Specific Audience
- [ ] Self Introduction
- [ ] State Purpose:

- [ ] Call-To-Action:

- [ ] Content:

- [ ] Ending:

- [ ] Take-Away:

- [ ] Call-To-Action:

- [ ] Thank
- [ ] Invite Back
- [ ] Contact Info
- [ ] Sign Off
- [ ] **Outro Cards**

Title: _____

Pre-Production
- ❏ topics ↠ outline ↠ script
- ❏ SEO research

Production
- ❏ prep set
- ❏ film movie
- ❏ film b-roll
- ❏ create thumbnail
- ❏ crate social media content

Post-Production
- ❏ edit: lighting
- ❏ edit: transitions
- ❏ edit: sound
- ❏ insert: branded intro
- ❏ insert: branded outro
- ❏ rename video file + thumbnail for upload

Upload
- ❏ SEO + LSI keywords
- ❏ front load keywords in title
- ❏ create description
- ❏ top tags (top channel names as last keywords)
- ❏ create time stamps for long videos
- ❏ add video to playlists
- ❏ monetize + categorize
- ❏ add social hook
- ❏ add end screens + cards

Engagement
- ❏ like + comment on video
- ❏ share to all social media
- ❏ comment on related content

Outline: What's my angle?

- [ ] First 15 Seconds:

- [ ] **Branded Intro**
- [ ] Greet Specific Audience
- [ ] Self Introduction
- [ ] State Purpose:

- [ ] Call-To-Action:

- [ ] Content:

- [ ] Ending:

- [ ] Take-Away:

- [ ] Call-To-Action:

- [ ] Thank
- [ ] Invite Back
- [ ] Contact Info
- [ ] Sign Off
- [ ] **Outro Cards**

Title: _____

Pre-Production
- ❏ topics » outline » script
- ❏ SEO research

Production
- ❏ prep set
- ❏ film movie
- ❏ film b-roll
- ❏ create thumbnail
- ❏ crate social media content

Post-Production
- ❏ edit: lighting
- ❏ edit: transitions
- ❏ edit: sound
- ❏ insert: branded intro
- ❏ insert: branded outro
- ❏ rename video file + thumbnail for upload

Upload
- ❏ SEO + LSI keywords
- ❏ front load keywords in title
- ❏ create description
- ❏ top tags (top channel names as last keywords)
- ❏ create time stamps for long videos
- ❏ add video to playlists
- ❏ monetize + categorize
- ❏ add social hook
- ❏ add end screens + cards

Engagement
- ❏ like + comment on video
- ❏ share to all social media
- ❏ comment on related content

Outline: What's my angle?

- ❏ First 15 Seconds:

- ❏ **Branded Intro**
- ❏ Greet Specific Audience
- ❏ Self Introduction
- ❏ State Purpose:

- ❏ Call-To-Action:

- ❏ Content:

- ❏ Ending:

- ❏ Take-Away:

- ❏ Call-To-Action:

- ❏ Thank
- ❏ Invite Back
- ❏ Contact Info
- ❏ Sign Off
- ❏ **Outro Cards**

Title: _____

Pre-Production
- ❏ topics » outline » script
- ❏ SEO research

Production
- ❏ prep set
- ❏ film movie
- ❏ film b-roll
- ❏ create thumbnail
- ❏ crate social media content

Post-Production
- ❏ edit: lighting
- ❏ edit: transitions
- ❏ edit: sound
- ❏ insert: branded intro
- ❏ insert: branded outro
- ❏ rename video file + thumbnail for upload

Upload
- ❏ SEO + LSI keywords
- ❏ front load keywords in title
- ❏ create description
- ❏ top tags (top channel names as last keywords)
- ❏ create time stamps for long videos
- ❏ add video to playlists
- ❏ monetize + categorize
- ❏ add social hook
- ❏ add end screens + cards

Engagement
- ❏ like + comment on video
- ❏ share to all social media
- ❏ comment on related content

Outline: What's my angle?

- ❏ First 15 Seconds:

- ❏ **Branded Intro**
- ❏ Greet Specific Audience
- ❏ Self Introduction
- ❏ State Purpose:

- ❏ Call-To-Action:

- ❏ Content:

- ❏ Ending:

- ❏ Take-Away:

- ❏ Call-To-Action:

- ❏ Thank
- ❏ Invite Back
- ❏ Contact Info
- ❏ Sign Off
- ❏ **Outro Cards**

Title: _____

Pre-Production
- ❏ topics » outline » script
- ❏ SEO research

Production
- ❏ prep set
- ❏ film movie
- ❏ film b-roll
- ❏ create thumbnail
- ❏ crate social media content

Post-Production
- ❏ edit: lighting
- ❏ edit: transitions
- ❏ edit: sound
- ❏ insert: branded intro
- ❏ insert: branded outro
- ❏ rename video file + thumbnail for upload

Upload
- ❏ SEO + LSI keywords
- ❏ front load keywords in title
- ❏ create description
- ❏ top tags (top channel names as last keywords)
- ❏ create time stamps for long videos
- ❏ add video to playlists
- ❏ monetize + categorize
- ❏ add social hook
- ❏ add end screens + cards

Engagement
- ❏ like + comment on video
- ❏ share to all social media
- ❏ comment on related content

Outline: *What's my angle?*

- ❏ First 15 Seconds:

- ❏ **Branded Intro**
- ❏ Greet Specific Audience
- ❏ Self Introduction
- ❏ State Purpose:

- ❏ Call-To-Action:

- ❏ Content:

- ❏ Ending:

- ❏ Take-Away:

- ❏ Call-To-Action:

- ❏ Thank
- ❏ Invite Back
- ❏ Contact Info
- ❏ Sign Off
- ❏ **Outro Cards**

Title: _____

Pre-Production
- ❏ topics » outline » script
- ❏ SEO research

Production
- ❏ prep set
- ❏ film movie
- ❏ film b-roll
- ❏ create thumbnail
- ❏ crate social media content

Post-Production
- ❏ edit: lighting
- ❏ edit: transitions
- ❏ edit: sound
- ❏ insert: branded intro
- ❏ insert: branded outro
- ❏ rename video file + thumbnail for upload

Upload
- ❏ SEO + LSI keywords
- ❏ front load keywords in title
- ❏ create description
- ❏ top tags (top channel names as last keywords)
- ❏ create time stamps for long videos
- ❏ add video to playlists
- ❏ monetize + categorize
- ❏ add social hook
- ❏ add end screens + cards

Engagement
- ❏ like + comment on video
- ❏ share to all social media
- ❏ comment on related content

Outline: What's my angle?

- [ ] First 15 Seconds:

- [ ] **Branded Intro**
- [ ] Greet Specific Audience
- [ ] Self Introduction
- [ ] State Purpose:

- [ ] Call-To-Action:

- [ ] Content:

- [ ] Ending:

- [ ] Take-Away:

- [ ] Call-To-Action:

- [ ] Thank
- [ ] Invite Back
- [ ] Contact Info
- [ ] Sign Off
- [ ] **Outro Cards**

Title: _____

Pre-Production
- ❏ topics » outline » script
- ❏ SEO research

Production
- ❏ prep set
- ❏ film movie
- ❏ film b-roll
- ❏ create thumbnail
- ❏ crate social media content

Post-Production
- ❏ edit: lighting
- ❏ edit: transitions
- ❏ edit: sound
- ❏ insert: branded intro
- ❏ insert: branded outro
- ❏ rename video file + thumbnail for upload

Upload
- ❏ SEO + LSI keywords
- ❏ front load keywords in title
- ❏ create description
- ❏ top tags (top channel names as last keywords)
- ❏ create time stamps for long videos
- ❏ add video to playlists
- ❏ monetize + categorize
- ❏ add social hook
- ❏ add end screens + cards

Engagement
- ❏ like + comment on video
- ❏ share to all social media
- ❏ comment on related content

Outline: *What's my angle?*

- First 15 Seconds:

- **Branded Intro**
  - Greet Specific Audience
  - Self Introduction
  - State Purpose:

- Call-To-Action:

- Content:

- Ending:

- Take-Away:

- Call-To-Action:

- Thank
- Invite Back
- Contact Info
- Sign Off
- **Outro Cards**

Title: _____

Pre-Production
- ❏ topics » outline » script
- ❏ SEO research

Production
- ❏ prep set
- ❏ film movie
- ❏ film b-roll
- ❏ create thumbnail
- ❏ crate social media content

Post-Production
- ❏ edit: lighting
- ❏ edit: transitions
- ❏ edit: sound
- ❏ insert: branded intro
- ❏ insert: branded outro
- ❏ rename video file + thumbnail for upload

Upload
- ❏ SEO + LSI keywords
- ❏ front load keywords in title
- ❏ create description
- ❏ top tags (top channel names as last keywords)
- ❏ create time stamps for long videos
- ❏ add video to playlists
- ❏ monetize + categorize
- ❏ add social hook
- ❏ add end screens + cards

Engagement
- ❏ like + comment on video
- ❏ share to all social media
- ❏ comment on related content

Outline: What's my angle?

- [ ] First 15 Seconds:

- [ ] **Branded Intro**
- [ ] Greet Specific Audience
- [ ] Self Introduction
- [ ] State Purpose:

- [ ] Call-To-Action:

- [ ] Content:

- [ ] Ending:

- [ ] Take-Away:

- [ ] Call-To-Action:

- [ ] Thank
- [ ] Invite Back
- [ ] Contact Info
- [ ] Sign Off
- [ ] **Outro Cards**

Title: _____

Pre-Production
- [ ] topics » outline » script
- [ ] SEO research

Production
- [ ] prep set
- [ ] film movie
- [ ] film b-roll
- [ ] create thumbnail
- [ ] crate social media content

Post-Production
- [ ] edit: lighting
- [ ] edit: transitions
- [ ] edit: sound
- [ ] insert: branded intro
- [ ] insert: branded outro
- [ ] rename video file + thumbnail for upload

Upload
- [ ] SEO + LSI keywords
- [ ] front load keywords in title
- [ ] create description
- [ ] top tags (top channel names as last keywords)
- [ ] create time stamps for long videos
- [ ] add video to playlists
- [ ] monetize + categorize
- [ ] add social hook
- [ ] add end screens + cards

Engagement
- [ ] like + comment on video
- [ ] share to all social media
- [ ] comment on related content

Outline: What's my angle?

- [ ] First 15 Seconds:

- [ ] **Branded Intro**
- [ ] Greet Specific Audience
- [ ] Self Introduction
- [ ] State Purpose:

- [ ] Call-To-Action:

- [ ] Content:

- [ ] Ending:

- [ ] Take-Away:

- [ ] Call-To-Action:

- [ ] Thank
- [ ] Invite Back
- [ ] Contact Info
- [ ] Sign Off
- [ ] **Outro Cards**

Title: _____

Pre-Production
- [ ] topics » outline » script
- [ ] SEO research

Production
- [ ] prep set
- [ ] film movie
- [ ] film b-roll
- [ ] create thumbnail
- [ ] crate social media content

Post-Production
- [ ] edit: lighting
- [ ] edit: transitions
- [ ] edit: sound
- [ ] insert: branded intro
- [ ] insert: branded outro
- [ ] rename video file + thumbnail for upload

Upload
- [ ] SEO + LSI keywords
- [ ] front load keywords in title
- [ ] create description
- [ ] top tags (top channel names as last keywords)
- [ ] create time stamps for long videos
- [ ] add video to playlists
- [ ] monetize + categorize
- [ ] add social hook
- [ ] add end screens + cards

Engagement
- [ ] like + comment on video
- [ ] share to all social media
- [ ] comment on related content

Outline: What's my angle?

- [ ] First 15 Seconds:

- [ ] **Branded Intro**
- [ ] Greet Specific Audience
- [ ] Self Introduction
- [ ] State Purpose:

- [ ] Call-To-Action:

- [ ] Content:

- [ ] Ending:

- [ ] Take-Away:

- [ ] Call-To-Action:

- [ ] Thank
- [ ] Invite Back
- [ ] Contact Info
- [ ] Sign Off
- [ ] **Outro Cards**

Title: _____

Pre-Production
- ❏ topics » outline » script
- ❏ SEO research

Production
- ❏ prep set
- ❏ film movie
- ❏ film b-roll
- ❏ create thumbnail
- ❏ crate social media content

Post-Production
- ❏ edit: lighting
- ❏ edit: transitions
- ❏ edit: sound
- ❏ insert: branded intro
- ❏ insert: branded outro
- ❏ rename video file + thumbnail for upload

Upload
- ❏ SEO + LSI keywords
- ❏ front load keywords in title
- ❏ create description
- ❏ top tags (top channel names as last keywords)
- ❏ create time stamps for long videos
- ❏ add video to playlists
- ❏ monetize + categorize
- ❏ add social hook
- ❏ add end screens + cards

Engagement
- ❏ like + comment on video
- ❏ share to all social media
- ❏ comment on related content

Outline: What's my angle?

- [ ] First 15 Seconds:

- [ ] **Branded Intro**
- [ ] Greet Specific Audience
- [ ] Self Introduction
- [ ] State Purpose:

- [ ] Call-To-Action:

- [ ] Content:

- [ ] Ending:

- [ ] Take-Away:

- [ ] Call-To-Action:

- [ ] Thank
- [ ] Invite Back
- [ ] Contact Info
- [ ] Sign Off
- [ ] **Outro Cards**

Title: _____

Pre-Production
- ❑ topics » outline » script
- ❑ SEO research

Production
- ❑ prep set
- ❑ film movie
- ❑ film b-roll
- ❑ create thumbnail
- ❑ crate social media content

Post-Production
- ❑ edit: lighting
- ❑ edit: transitions
- ❑ edit: sound
- ❑ insert: branded intro
- ❑ insert: branded outro
- ❑ rename video file + thumbnail for upload

Upload
- ❑ SEO + LSI keywords
- ❑ front load keywords in title
- ❑ create description
- ❑ top tags (top channel names as last keywords)
- ❑ create time stamps for long videos
- ❑ add video to playlists
- ❑ monetize + categorize
- ❑ add social hook
- ❑ add end screens + cards

Engagement
- ❑ like + comment on video
- ❑ share to all social media
- ❑ comment on related content

Outline: What's my angle?

- [ ] First 15 Seconds:

- [ ] **Branded Intro**
- [ ] Greet Specific Audience
- [ ] Self Introduction
- [ ] State Purpose:

- [ ] Call-To-Action:

- [ ] Content:

- [ ] Ending:

- [ ] Take-Away:

- [ ] Call-To-Action:

- [ ] Thank
- [ ] Invite Back
- [ ] Contact Info
- [ ] Sign Off
- [ ] **Outro Cards**

Title: _____

Pre-Production
- ❏ topics » outline » script
- ❏ SEO research

Production
- ❏ prep set
- ❏ film movie
- ❏ film b-roll
- ❏ create thumbnail
- ❏ crate social media content

Post-Production
- ❏ edit: lighting
- ❏ edit: transitions
- ❏ edit: sound
- ❏ insert: branded intro
- ❏ insert: branded outro
- ❏ rename video file + thumbnail for upload

Upload
- ❏ SEO + LSI keywords
- ❏ front load keywords in title
- ❏ create description
- ❏ top tags (top channel names as last keywords)
- ❏ create time stamps for long videos
- ❏ add video to playlists
- ❏ monetize + categorize
- ❏ add social hook
- ❏ add end screens + cards

Engagement
- ❏ like + comment on video
- ❏ share to all social media
- ❏ comment on related content

Outline: What's my angle?

- [ ] First 15 Seconds:

- [ ] **Branded Intro**
- [ ] Greet Specific Audience
- [ ] Self Introduction
- [ ] State Purpose:

- [ ] Call-To-Action:

- [ ] Content:

- [ ] Ending:

- [ ] Take-Away:

- [ ] Call-To-Action:

- [ ] Thank
- [ ] Invite Back
- [ ] Contact Info
- [ ] Sign Off
- [ ] **Outro Cards**

Title: _____

Pre-Production
- ❏ topics » outline » script
- ❏ SEO research

Production
- ❏ prep set
- ❏ film movie
- ❏ film b-roll
- ❏ create thumbnail
- ❏ crate social media content

Post-Production
- ❏ edit: lighting
- ❏ edit: transitions
- ❏ edit: sound
- ❏ insert: branded intro
- ❏ insert: branded outro
- ❏ rename video file + thumbnail for upload

Upload
- ❏ SEO + LSI keywords
- ❏ front load keywords in title
- ❏ create description
- ❏ top tags (top channel names as last keywords)
- ❏ create time stamps for long videos
- ❏ add video to playlists
- ❏ monetize + categorize
- ❏ add social hook
- ❏ add end screens + cards

Engagement
- ❏ like + comment on video
- ❏ share to all social media
- ❏ comment on related content

Outline: *What's my angle?*

- ❏ First 15 Seconds:

- ❏ **Branded Intro**
- ❏ Greet Specific Audience
- ❏ Self Introduction
- ❏ State Purpose:

- ❏ Call-To-Action:

- ❏ Content:

- ❏ Ending:

- ❏ Take-Away:

- ❏ Call-To-Action:

- ❏ Thank
- ❏ Invite Back
- ❏ Contact Info
- ❏ Sign Off
- ❏ **Outro Cards**

Title: _____

Pre-Production
- ❏ topics ⇢ outline ⇢ script
- ❏ SEO research

Production
- ❏ prep set
- ❏ film movie
- ❏ film b-roll
- ❏ create thumbnail
- ❏ crate social media content

Post-Production
- ❏ edit: lighting
- ❏ edit: transitions
- ❏ edit: sound
- ❏ insert: branded intro
- ❏ insert: branded outro
- ❏ rename video file + thumbnail for upload

Upload
- ❏ SEO + LSI keywords
- ❏ front load keywords in title
- ❏ create description
- ❏ top tags (top channel names as last keywords)
- ❏ create time stamps for long videos
- ❏ add video to playlists
- ❏ monetize + categorize
- ❏ add social hook
- ❏ add end screens + cards

Engagement
- ❏ like + comment on video
- ❏ share to all social media
- ❏ comment on related content

Outline: What's my angle?

- [ ] First 15 Seconds:

- [ ] **Branded Intro**
- [ ] Greet Specific Audience
- [ ] Self Introduction
- [ ] State Purpose:

- [ ] Call-To-Action:

- [ ] Content:

- [ ] Ending:

- [ ] Take-Away:

- [ ] Call-To-Action:

- [ ] Thank
- [ ] Invite Back
- [ ] Contact Info
- [ ] Sign Off
- [ ] **Outro Cards**

Title: _____

Pre-Production
- [ ] topics ↠ outline ↠ script
- [ ] SEO research

Production
- [ ] prep set
- [ ] film movie
- [ ] film b-roll
- [ ] create thumbnail
- [ ] crate social media content

Post-Production
- [ ] edit: lighting
- [ ] edit: transitions
- [ ] edit: sound
- [ ] insert: branded intro
- [ ] insert: branded outro
- [ ] rename video file + thumbnail for upload

Upload
- [ ] SEO + LSI keywords
- [ ] front load keywords in title
- [ ] create description
- [ ] top tags (top channel names as last keywords)
- [ ] create time stamps for long videos
- [ ] add video to playlists
- [ ] monetize + categorize
- [ ] add social hook
- [ ] add end screens + cards

Engagement
- [ ] like + comment on video
- [ ] share to all social media
- [ ] comment on related content

Outline: What's my angle?

- [ ] First 15 Seconds:

- [ ] **Branded Intro**
  - [ ] Greet Specific Audience
  - [ ] Self Introduction
  - [ ] State Purpose:

- [ ] Call-To-Action:

- [ ] Content:

- [ ] Ending:

- [ ] Take-Away:

- [ ] Call-To-Action:

- [ ] Thank
- [ ] Invite Back
- [ ] Contact Info
- [ ] Sign Off
- [ ] **Outro Cards**

Title: _____

Pre-Production
- ❏ topics ↠ outline ↠ script
- ❏ SEO research

Production
- ❏ prep set
- ❏ film movie
- ❏ film b-roll
- ❏ create thumbnail
- ❏ crate social media content

Post-Production
- ❏ edit: lighting
- ❏ edit: transitions
- ❏ edit: sound
- ❏ insert: branded intro
- ❏ insert: branded outro
- ❏ rename video file + thumbnail for upload

Upload
- ❏ SEO + LSI keywords
- ❏ front load keywords in title
- ❏ create description
- ❏ top tags (top channel names as last keywords)
- ❏ create time stamps for long videos
- ❏ add video to playlists
- ❏ monetize + categorize
- ❏ add social hook
- ❏ add end screens + cards

Engagement
- ❏ like + comment on video
- ❏ share to all social media
- ❏ comment on related content

Outline: What's my angle?

- ❏ First 15 Seconds:

- ❏ **Branded Intro**
- ❏ Greet Specific Audience
- ❏ Self Introduction
- ❏ State Purpose:

- ❏ Call-To-Action:

- ❏ Content:

- ❏ Ending:

- ❏ Take-Away:

- ❏ Call-To-Action:

- ❏ Thank
- ❏ Invite Back
- ❏ Contact Info
- ❏ Sign Off
- ❏ **Outro Cards**

Title: _____

Pre-Production
- ☐ topics » outline » script
- ☐ SEO research

Production
- ☐ prep set
- ☐ film movie
- ☐ film b-roll
- ☐ create thumbnail
- ☐ crate social media content

Post-Production
- ☐ edit: lighting
- ☐ edit: transitions
- ☐ edit: sound
- ☐ insert: branded intro
- ☐ insert: branded outro
- ☐ rename video file + thumbnail for upload

Upload
- ☐ SEO + LSI keywords
- ☐ front load keywords in title
- ☐ create description
- ☐ top tags (top channel names as last keywords)
- ☐ create time stamps for long videos
- ☐ add video to playlists
- ☐ monetize + categorize
- ☐ add social hook
- ☐ add end screens + cards

Engagement
- ☐ like + comment on video
- ☐ share to all social media
- ☐ comment on related content

Outline: What's my angle?

- [ ] First 15 Seconds:

- [ ] **Branded Intro**
- [ ] Greet Specific Audience
- [ ] Self Introduction
- [ ] State Purpose:

- [ ] Call-To-Action:

- [ ] Content:

- [ ] Ending:

- [ ] Take-Away:

- [ ] Call-To-Action:

- [ ] Thank
- [ ] Invite Back
- [ ] Contact Info
- [ ] Sign Off
- [ ] **Outro Cards**

Title: _____

Pre-Production
- ❏ topics » outline » script
- ❏ SEO research

Production
- ❏ prep set
- ❏ film movie
- ❏ film b-roll
- ❏ create thumbnail
- ❏ crate social media content

Post-Production
- ❏ edit: lighting
- ❏ edit: transitions
- ❏ edit: sound
- ❏ insert: branded intro
- ❏ insert: branded outro
- ❏ rename video file + thumbnail for upload

Upload
- ❏ SEO + LSI keywords
- ❏ front load keywords in title
- ❏ create description
- ❏ top tags (top channel names as last keywords)
- ❏ create time stamps for long videos
- ❏ add video to playlists
- ❏ monetize + categorize
- ❏ add social hook
- ❏ add end screens + cards

Engagement
- ❏ like + comment on video
- ❏ share to all social media
- ❏ comment on related content

Outline: What's my angle?

- [ ] First 15 Seconds:

- [ ] **Branded Intro**
- [ ] Greet Specific Audience
- [ ] Self Introduction
- [ ] State Purpose:

- [ ] Call-To-Action:

- [ ] Content:

- [ ] Ending:

- [ ] Take-Away:

- [ ] Call-To-Action:

- [ ] Thank
- [ ] Invite Back
- [ ] Contact Info
- [ ] Sign Off
- [ ] **Outro Cards**

Title: _____

Pre-Production
- ❏ topics ↠ outline ↠ script
- ❏ SEO research

Production
- ❏ prep set
- ❏ film movie
- ❏ film b-roll
- ❏ create thumbnail
- ❏ crate social media content

Post-Production
- ❏ edit: lighting
- ❏ edit: transitions
- ❏ edit: sound
- ❏ insert: branded intro
- ❏ insert: branded outro
- ❏ rename video file + thumbnail for upload

Upload
- ❏ SEO + LSI keywords
- ❏ front load keywords in title
- ❏ create description
- ❏ top tags (top channel names as last keywords)
- ❏ create time stamps for long videos
- ❏ add video to playlists
- ❏ monetize + categorize
- ❏ add social hook
- ❏ add end screens + cards

Engagement
- ❏ like + comment on video
- ❏ share to all social media
- ❏ comment on related content

Outline: *What's my angle?*

- [ ] First 15 Seconds:

- [ ] **Branded Intro**
- [ ] Greet Specific Audience
- [ ] Self Introduction
- [ ] State Purpose:

- [ ] Call-To-Action:

- [ ] Content:

- [ ] Ending:

- [ ] Take-Away:

- [ ] Call-To-Action:

- [ ] Thank
- [ ] Invite Back
- [ ] Contact Info
- [ ] Sign Off
- [ ] **Outro Cards**

Title: _____

Pre-Production
- ❑ topics » outline » script
- ❑ SEO research

Production
- ❑ prep set
- ❑ film movie
- ❑ film b-roll
- ❑ create thumbnail
- ❑ crate social media content

Post-Production
- ❑ edit: lighting
- ❑ edit: transitions
- ❑ edit: sound
- ❑ insert: branded intro
- ❑ insert: branded outro
- ❑ rename video file + thumbnail for upload

Upload
- ❑ SEO + LSI keywords
- ❑ front load keywords in title
- ❑ create description
- ❑ top tags (top channel names as last keywords)
- ❑ create time stamps for long videos
- ❑ add video to playlists
- ❑ monetize + categorize
- ❑ add social hook
- ❑ add end screens + cards

Engagement
- ❑ like + comment on video
- ❑ share to all social media
- ❑ comment on related content

Outline: *What's my angle?*

- [ ] First 15 Seconds:

- [ ] **Branded Intro**
- [ ] Greet Specific Audience
- [ ] Self Introduction
- [ ] State Purpose:

- [ ] Call-To-Action:

- [ ] Content:

- [ ] Ending:

- [ ] Take-Away:

- [ ] Call-To-Action:

- [ ] Thank
- [ ] Invite Back
- [ ] Contact Info
- [ ] Sign Off
- [ ] **Outro Cards**

Title: _____

Pre-Production
- ☐ topics » outline » script
- ☐ SEO research

Production
- ☐ prep set
- ☐ film movie
- ☐ film b-roll
- ☐ create thumbnail
- ☐ crate social media content

Post-Production
- ☐ edit: lighting
- ☐ edit: transitions
- ☐ edit: sound
- ☐ insert: branded intro
- ☐ insert: branded outro
- ☐ rename video file + thumbnail for upload

Upload
- ☐ SEO + LSI keywords
- ☐ front load keywords in title
- ☐ create description
- ☐ top tags (top channel names as last keywords)
- ☐ create time stamps for long videos
- ☐ add video to playlists
- ☐ monetize + categorize
- ☐ add social hook
- ☐ add end screens + cards

Engagement
- ☐ like + comment on video
- ☐ share to all social media
- ☐ comment on related content

Outline: *What's my angle?*

- [ ] First 15 Seconds:

- [ ] **Branded Intro**
  - [ ] Greet Specific Audience
  - [ ] Self Introduction
  - [ ] State Purpose:

- [ ] Call-To-Action:

- [ ] Content:

- [ ] Ending:

- [ ] Take-Away:

- [ ] Call-To-Action:

- [ ] Thank
- [ ] Invite Back
- [ ] Contact Info
- [ ] Sign Off
- [ ] **Outro Cards**

Title: _____

Pre-Production
- ❏ topics ↠ outline ↠ script
- ❏ SEO research

Production
- ❏ prep set
- ❏ film movie
- ❏ film b-roll
- ❏ create thumbnail
- ❏ crate social media content

Post-Production
- ❏ edit: lighting
- ❏ edit: transitions
- ❏ edit: sound
- ❏ insert: branded intro
- ❏ insert: branded outro
- ❏ rename video file + thumbnail for upload

Upload
- ❏ SEO + LSI keywords
- ❏ front load keywords in title
- ❏ create description
- ❏ top tags (top channel names as last keywords)
- ❏ create time stamps for long videos
- ❏ add video to playlists
- ❏ monetize + categorize
- ❏ add social hook
- ❏ add end screens + cards

Engagement
- ❏ like + comment on video
- ❏ share to all social media
- ❏ comment on related content

Outline: What's my angle?

❏ First 15 Seconds:

❏ **Branded Intro**
❏ Greet Specific Audience
❏ Self Introduction
❏ State Purpose:

❏ Call-To-Action:

❏ Content:

❏ Ending:

❏ Take-Away:

❏ Call-To-Action:

❏ Thank
❏ Invite Back
❏ Contact Info
❏ Sign Off
❏ **Outro Cards**

Title: _____

Pre-Production
- ❏ topics » outline » script
- ❏ SEO research

Production
- ❏ prep set
- ❏ film movie
- ❏ film b-roll
- ❏ create thumbnail
- ❏ crate social media content

Post-Production
- ❏ edit: lighting
- ❏ edit: transitions
- ❏ edit: sound
- ❏ insert: branded intro
- ❏ insert: branded outro
- ❏ rename video file + thumbnail for upload

Upload
- ❏ SEO + LSI keywords
- ❏ front load keywords in title
- ❏ create description
- ❏ top tags (top channel names as last keywords)
- ❏ create time stamps for long videos
- ❏ add video to playlists
- ❏ monetize + categorize
- ❏ add social hook
- ❏ add end screens + cards

Engagement
- ❏ like + comment on video
- ❏ share to all social media
- ❏ comment on related content

Outline: *What's my angle?*

- ❏ First 15 Seconds:

- ❏ **Branded Intro**
- ❏ Greet Specific Audience
- ❏ Self Introduction
- ❏ State Purpose:

- ❏ Call-To-Action:

- ❏ Content:

- ❏ Ending:

- ❏ Take-Away:

- ❏ Call-To-Action:

- ❏ Thank
- ❏ Invite Back
- ❏ Contact Info
- ❏ Sign Off
- ❏ **Outro Cards**

Title: _____

Pre-Production
- ☐ topics » outline » script
- ☐ SEO research

Production
- ☐ prep set
- ☐ film movie
- ☐ film b-roll
- ☐ create thumbnail
- ☐ crate social media content

Post-Production
- ☐ edit: lighting
- ☐ edit: transitions
- ☐ edit: sound
- ☐ insert: branded intro
- ☐ insert: branded outro
- ☐ rename video file + thumbnail for upload

Upload
- ☐ SEO + LSI keywords
- ☐ front load keywords in title
- ☐ create description
- ☐ top tags (top channel names as last keywords)
- ☐ create time stamps for long videos
- ☐ add video to playlists
- ☐ monetize + categorize
- ☐ add social hook
- ☐ add end screens + cards

Engagement
- ☐ like + comment on video
- ☐ share to all social media
- ☐ comment on related content

Outline: What's my angle?

- First 15 Seconds:

- **Branded Intro**
- Greet Specific Audience
- Self Introduction
- State Purpose:

- Call-To-Action:

- Content:

- Ending:

- Take-Away:

- Call-To-Action:

- Thank
- Invite Back
- Contact Info
- Sign Off
- **Outro Cards**

Title: _____

Pre-Production
- ❏ topics → outline → script
- ❏ SEO research

Production
- ❏ prep set
- ❏ film movie
- ❏ film b-roll
- ❏ create thumbnail
- ❏ crate social media content

Post-Production
- ❏ edit: lighting
- ❏ edit: transitions
- ❏ edit: sound
- ❏ insert: branded intro
- ❏ insert: branded outro
- ❏ rename video file + thumbnail for upload

Upload
- ❏ SEO + LSI keywords
- ❏ front load keywords in title
- ❏ create description
- ❏ top tags (top channel names as last keywords)
- ❏ create time stamps for long videos
- ❏ add video to playlists
- ❏ monetize + categorize
- ❏ add social hook
- ❏ add end screens + cards

Engagement
- ❏ like + comment on video
- ❏ share to all social media
- ❏ comment on related content

Outline: What's my angle?

- [ ] First 15 Seconds:

- [ ] **Branded Intro**
- [ ] Greet Specific Audience
- [ ] Self Introduction
- [ ] State Purpose:

- [ ] Call-To-Action:

- [ ] Content:

- [ ] Ending:

- [ ] Take-Away:

- [ ] Call-To-Action:

- [ ] Thank
- [ ] Invite Back
- [ ] Contact Info
- [ ] Sign Off
- [ ] **Outro Cards**

Title: _____

Pre-Production
- ❏ topics » outline » script
- ❏ SEO research

Production
- ❏ prep set
- ❏ film movie
- ❏ film b-roll
- ❏ create thumbnail
- ❏ crate social media content

Post-Production
- ❏ edit: lighting
- ❏ edit: transitions
- ❏ edit: sound
- ❏ insert: branded intro
- ❏ insert: branded outro
- ❏ rename video file + thumbnail for upload

Upload
- ❏ SEO + LSI keywords
- ❏ front load keywords in title
- ❏ create description
- ❏ top tags (top channel names as last keywords)
- ❏ create time stamps for long videos
- ❏ add video to playlists
- ❏ monetize + categorize
- ❏ add social hook
- ❏ add end screens + cards

Engagement
- ❏ like + comment on video
- ❏ share to all social media
- ❏ comment on related content

Outline: What's my angle?

- ❏ First 15 Seconds:

- ❏ **Branded Intro**
- ❏ Greet Specific Audience
- ❏ Self Introduction
- ❏ State Purpose:

- ❏ Call-To-Action:

- ❏ Content:

- ❏ Ending:

- ❏ Take-Away:

- ❏ Call-To-Action:

- ❏ Thank
- ❏ Invite Back
- ❏ Contact Info
- ❏ Sign Off
- ❏ **Outro Cards**

Title: _____

Pre-Production
- [ ] topics ↠ outline ↠ script
- [ ] SEO research

Production
- [ ] prep set
- [ ] film movie
- [ ] film b-roll
- [ ] create thumbnail
- [ ] crate social media content

Post-Production
- [ ] edit: lighting
- [ ] edit: transitions
- [ ] edit: sound
- [ ] insert: branded intro
- [ ] insert: branded outro
- [ ] rename video file + thumbnail for upload

Upload
- [ ] SEO + LSI keywords
- [ ] front load keywords in title
- [ ] create description
- [ ] top tags (top channel names as last keywords)
- [ ] create time stamps for long videos
- [ ] add video to playlists
- [ ] monetize + categorize
- [ ] add social hook
- [ ] add end screens + cards

Engagement
- [ ] like + comment on video
- [ ] share to all social media
- [ ] comment on related content

Outline: What's my angle?

- ❏ First 15 Seconds:

- ❏ **Branded Intro**
- ❏ Greet Specific Audience
- ❏ Self Introduction
- ❏ State Purpose:

- ❏ Call-To-Action:

- ❏ Content:

- ❏ Ending:

- ❏ Take-Away:

- ❏ Call-To-Action:

- ❏ Thank
- ❏ Invite Back
- ❏ Contact Info
- ❏ Sign Off
- ❏ **Outro Cards**

Title: _____

Pre-Production
- ❏ topics » outline » script
- ❏ SEO research

Production
- ❏ prep set
- ❏ film movie
- ❏ film b-roll
- ❏ create thumbnail
- ❏ crate social media content

Post-Production
- ❏ edit: lighting
- ❏ edit: transitions
- ❏ edit: sound
- ❏ insert: branded intro
- ❏ insert: branded outro
- ❏ rename video file + thumbnail for upload

Upload
- ❏ SEO + LSI keywords
- ❏ front load keywords in title
- ❏ create description
- ❏ top tags (top channel names as last keywords)
- ❏ create time stamps for long videos
- ❏ add video to playlists
- ❏ monetize + categorize
- ❏ add social hook
- ❏ add end screens + cards

Engagement
- ❏ like + comment on video
- ❏ share to all social media
- ❏ comment on related content

Outline: What's my angle?

- [ ] First 15 Seconds:

- [ ] **Branded Intro**
- [ ] Greet Specific Audience
- [ ] Self Introduction
- [ ] State Purpose:

- [ ] Call-To-Action:

- [ ] Content:

- [ ] Ending:

- [ ] Take-Away:

- [ ] Call-To-Action:

- [ ] Thank
- [ ] Invite Back
- [ ] Contact Info
- [ ] Sign Off
- [ ] **Outro Cards**

Title: _____

Pre-Production
- ❏ topics » outline » script
- ❏ SEO research

Production
- ❏ prep set
- ❏ film movie
- ❏ film b-roll
- ❏ create thumbnail
- ❏ crate social media content

Post-Production
- ❏ edit: lighting
- ❏ edit: transitions
- ❏ edit: sound
- ❏ insert: branded intro
- ❏ insert: branded outro
- ❏ rename video file + thumbnail for upload

Upload
- ❏ SEO + LSI keywords
- ❏ front load keywords in title
- ❏ create description
- ❏ top tags (top channel names as last keywords)
- ❏ create time stamps for long videos
- ❏ add video to playlists
- ❏ monetize + categorize
- ❏ add social hook
- ❏ add end screens + cards

Engagement
- ❏ like + comment on video
- ❏ share to all social media
- ❏ comment on related content

Outline: What's my angle?

- [ ] First 15 Seconds:

- [ ] **Branded Intro**
- [ ] Greet Specific Audience
- [ ] Self Introduction
- [ ] State Purpose:

- [ ] Call-To-Action:

- [ ] Content:

- [ ] Ending:

- [ ] Take-Away:

- [ ] Call-To-Action:

- [ ] Thank
- [ ] Invite Back
- [ ] Contact Info
- [ ] Sign Off
- [ ] **Outro Cards**

Title: _____

Pre-Production
- ❏ topics » outline » script
- ❏ SEO research

Production
- ❏ prep set
- ❏ film movie
- ❏ film b-roll
- ❏ create thumbnail
- ❏ crate social media content

Post-Production
- ❏ edit: lighting
- ❏ edit: transitions
- ❏ edit: sound
- ❏ insert: branded intro
- ❏ insert: branded outro
- ❏ rename video file + thumbnail for upload

Upload
- ❏ SEO + LSI keywords
- ❏ front load keywords in title
- ❏ create description
- ❏ top tags (top channel names as last keywords)
- ❏ create time stamps for long videos
- ❏ add video to playlists
- ❏ monetize + categorize
- ❏ add social hook
- ❏ add end screens + cards

Engagement
- ❏ like + comment on video
- ❏ share to all social media
- ❏ comment on related content

Outline: What's my angle?

- First 15 Seconds:

- **Branded Intro**
- Greet Specific Audience
- Self Introduction
- State Purpose:

- Call-To-Action:

- Content:

- Ending:

- Take-Away:

- Call-To-Action:

- Thank
- Invite Back
- Contact Info
- Sign Off
- **Outro Cards**

Title: _____

Pre-Production
- ❏ topics » outline » script
- ❏ SEO research

Production
- ❏ prep set
- ❏ film movie
- ❏ film b-roll
- ❏ create thumbnail
- ❏ crate social media content

Post-Production
- ❏ edit: lighting
- ❏ edit: transitions
- ❏ edit: sound
- ❏ insert: branded intro
- ❏ insert: branded outro
- ❏ rename video file + thumbnail for upload

Upload
- ❏ SEO + LSI keywords
- ❏ front load keywords in title
- ❏ create description
- ❏ top tags (top channel names as last keywords)
- ❏ create time stamps for long videos
- ❏ add video to playlists
- ❏ monetize + categorize
- ❏ add social hook
- ❏ add end screens + cards

Engagement
- ❏ like + comment on video
- ❏ share to all social media
- ❏ comment on related content

Outline: *What's my angle?*

- ❏ First 15 Seconds:

- ❏ **Branded Intro**
- ❏ Greet Specific Audience
- ❏ Self Introduction
- ❏ State Purpose:

- ❏ Call-To-Action:

- ❏ Content:

- ❏ Ending:

- ❏ Take-Away:

- ❏ Call-To-Action:

- ❏ Thank
- ❏ Invite Back
- ❏ Contact Info
- ❏ Sign Off
- ❏ **Outro Cards**

Title: _____

Pre-Production
- ❏ topics » outline » script
- ❏ SEO research

Production
- ❏ prep set
- ❏ film movie
- ❏ film b-roll
- ❏ create thumbnail
- ❏ crate social media content

Post-Production
- ❏ edit: lighting
- ❏ edit: transitions
- ❏ edit: sound
- ❏ insert: branded intro
- ❏ insert: branded outro
- ❏ rename video file + thumbnail for upload

Upload
- ❏ SEO + LSI keywords
- ❏ front load keywords in title
- ❏ create description
- ❏ top tags (top channel names as last keywords)
- ❏ create time stamps for long videos
- ❏ add video to playlists
- ❏ monetize + categorize
- ❏ add social hook
- ❏ add end screens + cards

Engagement
- ❏ like + comment on video
- ❏ share to all social media
- ❏ comment on related content

Outline: *What's my angle?*

- ❏ First 15 Seconds:

- ❏ **Branded Intro**
  - ❏ Greet Specific Audience
  - ❏ Self Introduction
  - ❏ State Purpose:

- ❏ Call-To-Action:

- ❏ Content:

- ❏ Ending:

- ❏ Take-Away:

- ❏ Call-To-Action:

- ❏ Thank
- ❏ Invite Back
- ❏ Contact Info
- ❏ Sign Off
- ❏ **Outro Cards**

Title: _____

Pre-Production
- ☐ topics » outline » script
- ☐ SEO research

Production
- ☐ prep set
- ☐ film movie
- ☐ film b-roll
- ☐ create thumbnail
- ☐ crate social media content

Post-Production
- ☐ edit: lighting
- ☐ edit: transitions
- ☐ edit: sound
- ☐ insert: branded intro
- ☐ insert: branded outro
- ☐ rename video file + thumbnail for upload

Upload
- ☐ SEO + LSI keywords
- ☐ front load keywords in title
- ☐ create description
- ☐ top tags (top channel names as last keywords)
- ☐ create time stamps for long videos
- ☐ add video to playlists
- ☐ monetize + categorize
- ☐ add social hook
- ☐ add end screens + cards

Engagement
- ☐ like + comment on video
- ☐ share to all social media
- ☐ comment on related content

Outline: What's my angle?

- ❏ First 15 Seconds:

- ❏ **Branded Intro**
- ❏ Greet Specific Audience
- ❏ Self Introduction
- ❏ State Purpose:

- ❏ Call-To-Action:

- ❏ Content:

- ❏ Ending:

- ❏ Take-Away:

- ❏ Call-To-Action:

- ❏ Thank
- ❏ Invite Back
- ❏ Contact Info
- ❏ Sign Off
- ❏ **Outro Cards**

Title: _____

Pre-Production
- ❏ topics → outline → script
- ❏ SEO research

Production
- ❏ prep set
- ❏ film movie
- ❏ film b-roll
- ❏ create thumbnail
- ❏ crate social media content

Post-Production
- ❏ edit: lighting
- ❏ edit: transitions
- ❏ edit: sound
- ❏ insert: branded intro
- ❏ insert: branded outro
- ❏ rename video file + thumbnail for upload

Upload
- ❏ SEO + LSI keywords
- ❏ front load keywords in title
- ❏ create description
- ❏ top tags (top channel names as last keywords)
- ❏ create time stamps for long videos
- ❏ add video to playlists
- ❏ monetize + categorize
- ❏ add social hook
- ❏ add end screens + cards

Engagement
- ❏ like + comment on video
- ❏ share to all social media
- ❏ comment on related content

Outline: What's my angle?

- ❏ First 15 Seconds:

- ❏ **Branded Intro**
  - ❏ Greet Specific Audience
  - ❏ Self Introduction
  - ❏ State Purpose:

- ❏ Call-To-Action:

- ❏ Content:

- ❏ Ending:

- ❏ Take-Away:

- ❏ Call-To-Action:

- ❏ Thank
- ❏ Invite Back
- ❏ Contact Info
- ❏ Sign Off
- ❏ **Outro Cards**

Title: _____

Pre-Production
- ❏ topics » outline » script
- ❏ SEO research

Production
- ❏ prep set
- ❏ film movie
- ❏ film b-roll
- ❏ create thumbnail
- ❏ crate social media content

Post-Production
- ❏ edit: lighting
- ❏ edit: transitions
- ❏ edit: sound
- ❏ insert: branded intro
- ❏ insert: branded outro
- ❏ rename video file + thumbnail for upload

Upload
- ❏ SEO + LSI keywords
- ❏ front load keywords in title
- ❏ create description
- ❏ top tags (top channel names as last keywords)
- ❏ create time stamps for long videos
- ❏ add video to playlists
- ❏ monetize + categorize
- ❏ add social hook
- ❏ add end screens + cards

Engagement
- ❏ like + comment on video
- ❏ share to all social media
- ❏ comment on related content

Outline: What's my angle?

- [ ] First 15 Seconds:

- [ ] **Branded Intro**
  - [ ] Greet Specific Audience
  - [ ] Self Introduction
  - [ ] State Purpose:

- [ ] Call-To-Action:

- [ ] Content:

- [ ] Ending:

- [ ] Take-Away:

- [ ] Call-To-Action:

- [ ] Thank
- [ ] Invite Back
- [ ] Contact Info
- [ ] Sign Off
- [ ] **Outro Cards**

Title: _____

PRE-PRODUCTION
- ❏ topics » outline » script
- ❏ SEO research

PRODUCTION
- ❏ prep set
- ❏ film movie
- ❏ film b-roll
- ❏ create thumbnail
- ❏ crate social media content

POST-PRODUCTION
- ❏ edit: lighting
- ❏ edit: transitions
- ❏ edit: sound
- ❏ insert: branded intro
- ❏ insert: branded outro
- ❏ rename video file + thumbnail for upload

UPLOAD
- ❏ SEO + LSI keywords
- ❏ front load keywords in title
- ❏ create description
- ❏ top tags (top channel names as last keywords)
- ❏ create time stamps for long videos
- ❏ add video to playlists
- ❏ monetize + categorize
- ❏ add social hook
- ❏ add end screens + cards

ENGAGEMENT
- ❏ like + comment on video
- ❏ share to all social media
- ❏ comment on related content

Outline: *What's my angle?*

- ☐ First 15 Seconds:

- ☐ **Branded Intro**
- ☐ Greet Specific Audience
- ☐ Self Introduction
- ☐ State Purpose:

- ☐ Call-To-Action:

- ☐ Content:

- ☐ Ending:

- ☐ Take-Away:

- ☐ Call-To-Action:

- ☐ Thank
- ☐ Invite Back
- ☐ Contact Info
- ☐ Sign Off
- ☐ **Outro Cards**

Title: _____

Pre-Production
- ❏ topics ↠ outline ↠ script
- ❏ SEO research

Production
- ❏ prep set
- ❏ film movie
- ❏ film b-roll
- ❏ create thumbnail
- ❏ crate social media content

Post-Production
- ❏ edit: lighting
- ❏ edit: transitions
- ❏ edit: sound
- ❏ insert: branded intro
- ❏ insert: branded outro
- ❏ rename video file + thumbnail for upload

Upload
- ❏ SEO + LSI keywords
- ❏ front load keywords in title
- ❏ create description
- ❏ top tags (top channel names as last keywords)
- ❏ create time stamps for long videos
- ❏ add video to playlists
- ❏ monetize + categorize
- ❏ add social hook
- ❏ add end screens + cards

Engagement
- ❏ like + comment on video
- ❏ share to all social media
- ❏ comment on related content

Outline: *What's my angle?*

- [ ] First 15 Seconds:

- [ ] **Branded Intro**
- [ ] Greet Specific Audience
- [ ] Self Introduction
- [ ] State Purpose:

- [ ] Call-To-Action:

- [ ] Content:

- [ ] Ending:

- [ ] Take-Away:

- [ ] Call-To-Action:

- [ ] Thank
- [ ] Invite Back
- [ ] Contact Info
- [ ] Sign Off
- [ ] **Outro Cards**

Title: _____

Pre-Production
- ❏ topics » outline » script
- ❏ SEO research

Production
- ❏ prep set
- ❏ film movie
- ❏ film b-roll
- ❏ create thumbnail
- ❏ crate social media content

Post-Production
- ❏ edit: lighting
- ❏ edit: transitions
- ❏ edit: sound
- ❏ insert: branded intro
- ❏ insert: branded outro
- ❏ rename video file + thumbnail for upload

Upload
- ❏ SEO + LSI keywords
- ❏ front load keywords in title
- ❏ create description
- ❏ top tags (top channel names as last keywords)
- ❏ create time stamps for long videos
- ❏ add video to playlists
- ❏ monetize + categorize
- ❏ add social hook
- ❏ add end screens + cards

Engagement
- ❏ like + comment on video
- ❏ share to all social media
- ❏ comment on related content

Outline: *What's my angle?*

- [ ] First 15 Seconds:

- [ ] **Branded Intro**
- [ ] Greet Specific Audience
- [ ] Self Introduction
- [ ] State Purpose:

- [ ] Call-To-Action:

- [ ] Content:

- [ ] Ending:

- [ ] Take-Away:

- [ ] Call-To-Action:

- [ ] Thank
- [ ] Invite Back
- [ ] Contact Info
- [ ] Sign Off
- [ ] **Outro Cards**

Title: _____

Pre-Production
- ☐ topics » outline » script
- ☐ SEO research

Production
- ☐ prep set
- ☐ film movie
- ☐ film b-roll
- ☐ create thumbnail
- ☐ crate social media content

Post-Production
- ☐ edit: lighting
- ☐ edit: transitions
- ☐ edit: sound
- ☐ insert: branded intro
- ☐ insert: branded outro
- ☐ rename video file + thumbnail for upload

Upload
- ☐ SEO + LSI keywords
- ☐ front load keywords in title
- ☐ create description
- ☐ top tags (top channel names as last keywords)
- ☐ create time stamps for long videos
- ☐ add video to playlists
- ☐ monetize + categorize
- ☐ add social hook
- ☐ add end screens + cards

Engagement
- ☐ like + comment on video
- ☐ share to all social media
- ☐ comment on related content

Outline: *What's my angle?*

- [ ] First 15 Seconds:

- [ ] **Branded Intro**
- [ ] Greet Specific Audience
- [ ] Self Introduction
- [ ] State Purpose:

- [ ] Call-To-Action:

- [ ] Content:

- [ ] Ending:

- [ ] Take-Away:

- [ ] Call-To-Action:

- [ ] Thank
- [ ] Invite Back
- [ ] Contact Info
- [ ] Sign Off
- [ ] **Outro Cards**

Title: _____

Pre-Production
- ❏ topics ↠ outline ↠ script
- ❏ SEO research

Production
- ❏ prep set
- ❏ film movie
- ❏ film b-roll
- ❏ create thumbnail
- ❏ crate social media content

Post-Production
- ❏ edit: lighting
- ❏ edit: transitions
- ❏ edit: sound
- ❏ insert: branded intro
- ❏ insert: branded outro
- ❏ rename video file + thumbnail for upload

Upload
- ❏ SEO + LSI keywords
- ❏ front load keywords in title
- ❏ create description
- ❏ top tags (top channel names as last keywords)
- ❏ create time stamps for long videos
- ❏ add video to playlists
- ❏ monetize + categorize
- ❏ add social hook
- ❏ add end screens + cards

Engagement
- ❏ like + comment on video
- ❏ share to all social media
- ❏ comment on related content

Outline: What's my angle?

- [ ] First 15 Seconds:

- [ ] **Branded Intro**
  - [ ] Greet Specific Audience
  - [ ] Self Introduction
  - [ ] State Purpose:

- [ ] Call-To-Action:

- [ ] Content:

- [ ] Ending:

- [ ] Take-Away:

- [ ] Call-To-Action:

- [ ] Thank
- [ ] Invite Back
- [ ] Contact Info
- [ ] Sign Off
- [ ] **Outro Cards**

Title: _____

Pre-Production
- ❏ topics » outline » script
- ❏ SEO research

Production
- ❏ prep set
- ❏ film movie
- ❏ film b-roll
- ❏ create thumbnail
- ❏ crate social media content

Post-Production
- ❏ edit: lighting
- ❏ edit: transitions
- ❏ edit: sound
- ❏ insert: branded intro
- ❏ insert: branded outro
- ❏ rename video file + thumbnail for upload

Upload
- ❏ SEO + LSI keywords
- ❏ front load keywords in title
- ❏ create description
- ❏ top tags (top channel names as last keywords)
- ❏ create time stamps for long videos
- ❏ add video to playlists
- ❏ monetize + categorize
- ❏ add social hook
- ❏ add end screens + cards

Engagement
- ❏ like + comment on video
- ❏ share to all social media
- ❏ comment on related content

Outline: *What's my angle?*

- ☐ First 15 Seconds:

- ☐ **Branded Intro**
- ☐ Greet Specific Audience
- ☐ Self Introduction
- ☐ State Purpose:

- ☐ Call-To-Action:

- ☐ Content:

- ☐ Ending:

- ☐ Take-Away:

- ☐ Call-To-Action:

- ☐ Thank
- ☐ Invite Back
- ☐ Contact Info
- ☐ Sign Off
- ☐ **Outro Cards**

Title: _____

Pre-Production
- ❏ topics » outline » script
- ❏ SEO research

Production
- ❏ prep set
- ❏ film movie
- ❏ film b-roll
- ❏ create thumbnail
- ❏ crate social media content

Post-Production
- ❏ edit: lighting
- ❏ edit: transitions
- ❏ edit: sound
- ❏ insert: branded intro
- ❏ insert: branded outro
- ❏ rename video file + thumbnail for upload

Upload
- ❏ SEO + LSI keywords
- ❏ front load keywords in title
- ❏ create description
- ❏ top tags (top channel names as last keywords)
- ❏ create time stamps for long videos
- ❏ add video to playlists
- ❏ monetize + categorize
- ❏ add social hook
- ❏ add end screens + cards

Engagement
- ❏ like + comment on video
- ❏ share to all social media
- ❏ comment on related content

Outline: What's my angle?

- [ ] First 15 Seconds:

- [ ] **Branded Intro**
  - [ ] Greet Specific Audience
  - [ ] Self Introduction
  - [ ] State Purpose:

- [ ] Call-To-Action:

- [ ] Content:

- [ ] Ending:

- [ ] Take-Away:

- [ ] Call-To-Action:

- [ ] Thank
- [ ] Invite Back
- [ ] Contact Info
- [ ] Sign Off
- [ ] **Outro Cards**

Title: _____

Pre-Production
- ❏ topics » outline » script
- ❏ SEO research

Production
- ❏ prep set
- ❏ film movie
- ❏ film b-roll
- ❏ create thumbnail
- ❏ crate social media content

Post-Production
- ❏ edit: lighting
- ❏ edit: transitions
- ❏ edit: sound
- ❏ insert: branded intro
- ❏ insert: branded outro
- ❏ rename video file + thumbnail for upload

Upload
- ❏ SEO + LSI keywords
- ❏ front load keywords in title
- ❏ create description
- ❏ top tags (top channel names as last keywords)
- ❏ create time stamps for long videos
- ❏ add video to playlists
- ❏ monetize + categorize
- ❏ add social hook
- ❏ add end screens + cards

Engagement
- ❏ like + comment on video
- ❏ share to all social media
- ❏ comment on related content

Outline: *What's my angle?*

- ❏ First 15 Seconds:

- ❏ **Branded Intro**
- ❏ Greet Specific Audience
- ❏ Self Introduction
- ❏ State Purpose:

- ❏ Call-To-Action:

- ❏ Content:

- ❏ Ending:

- ❏ Take-Away:

- ❏ Call-To-Action:

- ❏ Thank
- ❏ Invite Back
- ❏ Contact Info
- ❏ Sign Off
- ❏ **Outro Cards**

Title: _____

Pre-Production
- ❏ topics » outline » script
- ❏ SEO research

Production
- ❏ prep set
- ❏ film movie
- ❏ film b-roll
- ❏ create thumbnail
- ❏ crate social media content

Post-Production
- ❏ edit: lighting
- ❏ edit: transitions
- ❏ edit: sound
- ❏ insert: branded intro
- ❏ insert: branded outro
- ❏ rename video file + thumbnail for upload

Upload
- ❏ SEO + LSI keywords
- ❏ front load keywords in title
- ❏ create description
- ❏ top tags (top channel names as last keywords)
- ❏ create time stamps for long videos
- ❏ add video to playlists
- ❏ monetize + categorize
- ❏ add social hook
- ❏ add end screens + cards

Engagement
- ❏ like + comment on video
- ❏ share to all social media
- ❏ comment on related content

Outline: *What's my angle?*

- [ ] First 15 Seconds:

- [ ] **Branded Intro**
- [ ] Greet Specific Audience
- [ ] Self Introduction
- [ ] State Purpose:

- [ ] Call-To-Action:

- [ ] Content:

- [ ] Ending:

- [ ] Take-Away:

- [ ] Call-To-Action:

- [ ] Thank
- [ ] Invite Back
- [ ] Contact Info
- [ ] Sign Off
- [ ] **Outro Cards**

Title: _____

Pre-Production
- ❏ topics » outline » script
- ❏ SEO research

Production
- ❏ prep set
- ❏ film movie
- ❏ film b-roll
- ❏ create thumbnail
- ❏ crate social media content

Post-Production
- ❏ edit: lighting
- ❏ edit: transitions
- ❏ edit: sound
- ❏ insert: branded intro
- ❏ insert: branded outro
- ❏ rename video file + thumbnail for upload

Upload
- ❏ SEO + LSI keywords
- ❏ front load keywords in title
- ❏ create description
- ❏ top tags (top channel names as last keywords)
- ❏ create time stamps for long videos
- ❏ add video to playlists
- ❏ monetize + categorize
- ❏ add social hook
- ❏ add end screens + cards

Engagement
- ❏ like + comment on video
- ❏ share to all social media
- ❏ comment on related content

Outline: What's my angle?

- First 15 Seconds:

- **Branded Intro**
- Greet Specific Audience
- Self Introduction
- State Purpose:

- Call-To-Action:

- Content:

- Ending:

- Take-Away:

- Call-To-Action:

- Thank
- Invite Back
- Contact Info
- Sign Off
- **Outro Cards**

Title: _____

Pre-Production
- ❏ topics ›› outline ›› script
- ❏ SEO research

Production
- ❏ prep set
- ❏ film movie
- ❏ film b-roll
- ❏ create thumbnail
- ❏ crate social media content

Post-Production
- ❏ edit: lighting
- ❏ edit: transitions
- ❏ edit: sound
- ❏ insert: branded intro
- ❏ insert: branded outro
- ❏ rename video file + thumbnail for upload

Upload
- ❏ SEO + LSI keywords
- ❏ front load keywords in title
- ❏ create description
- ❏ top tags (top channel names as last keywords)
- ❏ create time stamps for long videos
- ❏ add video to playlists
- ❏ monetize + categorize
- ❏ add social hook
- ❏ add end screens + cards

Engagement
- ❏ like + comment on video
- ❏ share to all social media
- ❏ comment on related content

Outline: *What's my angle?*

- ❏ First 15 Seconds:

- ❏ **Branded Intro**
- ❏ Greet Specific Audience
- ❏ Self Introduction
- ❏ State Purpose:

- ❏ Call-To-Action:

- ❏ Content:

- ❏ Ending:

- ❏ Take-Away:

- ❏ Call-To-Action:

- ❏ Thank
- ❏ Invite Back
- ❏ Contact Info
- ❏ Sign Off
- ❏ **Outro Cards**

Title: _____

Pre-Production
- ❏ topics » outline » script
- ❏ SEO research

Production
- ❏ prep set
- ❏ film movie
- ❏ film b-roll
- ❏ create thumbnail
- ❏ crate social media content

Post-Production
- ❏ edit: lighting
- ❏ edit: transitions
- ❏ edit: sound
- ❏ insert: branded intro
- ❏ insert: branded outro
- ❏ rename video file + thumbnail for upload

Upload
- ❏ SEO + LSI keywords
- ❏ front load keywords in title
- ❏ create description
- ❏ top tags (top channel names as last keywords)
- ❏ create time stamps for long videos
- ❏ add video to playlists
- ❏ monetize + categorize
- ❏ add social hook
- ❏ add end screens + cards

Engagement
- ❏ like + comment on video
- ❏ share to all social media
- ❏ comment on related content

Outline: What's my angle?

- [ ] First 15 Seconds:

- [ ] **Branded Intro**
- [ ] Greet Specific Audience
- [ ] Self Introduction
- [ ] State Purpose:

- [ ] Call-To-Action:

- [ ] Content:

- [ ] Ending:

- [ ] Take-Away:

- [ ] Call-To-Action:

- [ ] Thank
- [ ] Invite Back
- [ ] Contact Info
- [ ] Sign Off
- [ ] **Outro Cards**

Title: _____

Pre-Production
- ❏ topics ⇾ outline ⇾ script
- ❏ SEO research

Production
- ❏ prep set
- ❏ film movie
- ❏ film b-roll
- ❏ create thumbnail
- ❏ crate social media content

Post-Production
- ❏ edit: lighting
- ❏ edit: transitions
- ❏ edit: sound
- ❏ insert: branded intro
- ❏ insert: branded outro
- ❏ rename video file + thumbnail for upload

Upload
- ❏ SEO + LSI keywords
- ❏ front load keywords in title
- ❏ create description
- ❏ top tags (top channel names as last keywords)
- ❏ create time stamps for long videos
- ❏ add video to playlists
- ❏ monetize + categorize
- ❏ add social hook
- ❏ add end screens + cards

Engagement
- ❏ like + comment on video
- ❏ share to all social media
- ❏ comment on related content

Outline: What's my angle?

- ☐ First 15 Seconds:

- ☐ **Branded Intro**
  - ☐ Greet Specific Audience
  - ☐ Self Introduction
  - ☐ State Purpose:

- ☐ Call-To-Action:

- ☐ Content:

- ☐ Ending:

- ☐ Take-Away:

- ☐ Call-To-Action:

- ☐ Thank
- ☐ Invite Back
- ☐ Contact Info
- ☐ Sign Off
- ☐ **Outro Cards**

Title: _____

Pre-Production
- ❏ topics » outline » script
- ❏ SEO research

Production
- ❏ prep set
- ❏ film movie
- ❏ film b-roll
- ❏ create thumbnail
- ❏ crate social media content

Post-Production
- ❏ edit: lighting
- ❏ edit: transitions
- ❏ edit: sound
- ❏ insert: branded intro
- ❏ insert: branded outro
- ❏ rename video file + thumbnail for upload

Upload
- ❏ SEO + LSI keywords
- ❏ front load keywords in title
- ❏ create description
- ❏ top tags (top channel names as last keywords)
- ❏ create time stamps for long videos
- ❏ add video to playlists
- ❏ monetize + categorize
- ❏ add social hook
- ❏ add end screens + cards

Engagement
- ❏ like + comment on video
- ❏ share to all social media
- ❏ comment on related content

Outline: *What's my angle?*

- ❏ First 15 Seconds:

- ❏ **Branded Intro**
- ❏ Greet Specific Audience
- ❏ Self Introduction
- ❏ State Purpose:

- ❏ Call-To-Action:

- ❏ Content:

- ❏ Ending:

- ❏ Take-Away:

- ❏ Call-To-Action:

- ❏ Thank
- ❏ Invite Back
- ❏ Contact Info
- ❏ Sign Off
- ❏ **Outro Cards**

Title: _____

Pre-Production
- ❏ topics » outline » script
- ❏ SEO research

Production
- ❏ prep set
- ❏ film movie
- ❏ film b-roll
- ❏ create thumbnail
- ❏ crate social media content

Post-Production
- ❏ edit: lighting
- ❏ edit: transitions
- ❏ edit: sound
- ❏ insert: branded intro
- ❏ insert: branded outro
- ❏ rename video file + thumbnail for upload

Upload
- ❏ SEO + LSI keywords
- ❏ front load keywords in title
- ❏ create description
- ❏ top tags (top channel names as last keywords)
- ❏ create time stamps for long videos
- ❏ add video to playlists
- ❏ monetize + categorize
- ❏ add social hook
- ❏ add end screens + cards

Engagement
- ❏ like + comment on video
- ❏ share to all social media
- ❏ comment on related content

Outline: What's my angle?

- [ ] First 15 Seconds:

- [ ] **Branded Intro**
- [ ] Greet Specific Audience
- [ ] Self Introduction
- [ ] State Purpose:

- [ ] Call-To-Action:

- [ ] Content:

- [ ] Ending:

- [ ] Take-Away:

- [ ] Call-To-Action:

- [ ] Thank
- [ ] Invite Back
- [ ] Contact Info
- [ ] Sign Off
- [ ] **Outro Cards**

Title: _____

Pre-Production
- ❏ topics » outline » script
- ❏ SEO research

Production
- ❏ prep set
- ❏ film movie
- ❏ film b-roll
- ❏ create thumbnail
- ❏ crate social media content

Post-Production
- ❏ edit: lighting
- ❏ edit: transitions
- ❏ edit: sound
- ❏ insert: branded intro
- ❏ insert: branded outro
- ❏ rename video file + thumbnail for upload

Upload
- ❏ SEO + LSI keywords
- ❏ front load keywords in title
- ❏ create description
- ❏ top tags (top channel names as last keywords)
- ❏ create time stamps for long videos
- ❏ add video to playlists
- ❏ monetize + categorize
- ❏ add social hook
- ❏ add end screens + cards

Engagement
- ❏ like + comment on video
- ❏ share to all social media
- ❏ comment on related content

Outline: What's my angle?

- First 15 Seconds:

- **Branded Intro**
  - Greet Specific Audience
  - Self Introduction
  - State Purpose:

- Call-To-Action:

- Content:

- Ending:

- Take-Away:

- Call-To-Action:

- Thank
- Invite Back
- Contact Info
- Sign Off
- **Outro Cards**

www.ingramcontent.com/pod-product-compliance
Lightning Source LLC
Chambersburg PA
CBHW071652240526
45469CB00021B/2268